CHOOSING
DEMOCRACY

What Is Democracy?

DEMOCRACY

Rebecca Sjonger

CRABTREE
PUBLISHING COMPANY
WWW.CRABTREEBOOKS.COM

CRABTREE
PUBLISHING COMPANY
WWW.CRABTREEBOOKS.COM

Author: Rebecca Sjonger
Series research and development:
 Janine Deschenes
Editors: Ellen Rodger, Janine Deschenes
Proofreader: Wendy Scavuzzo
Design and photo research: Katherine Berti
Print and production coordinator:
 Katherine Berti

Dedicated by Rebecca Sjonger:
For Carlie Sunshine,
whose future is bright!

Front cover: Free and
fair elections are one of
the cornerstones of a
healthy democracy. Here,
election officials check the
identification of people lined
up to vote at an Arlington,
Virgina, voting station.

Image credits:
Alamy Stock Photo
 REUTERS/Patrick Doyle: p. 33 (bottom left)
Flickr
 Province of British Columbia: p. 32 (top)
 Seattle Parks and Recreation: p. 34 (top right)
Government of Canada
 Reproduced with the permission of Library and
  Archives Canada (2021): p. 19
 © All rights reserved: Department of Canadian
  Heritage. Reproduced with the permission of
  the Minister of Canadian Heritage, 2021: p. 20
Shutterstock
 19bProduction: p. 44 (top)
 a katz: p. 29 (top)
 Alexander Khitrov: p. 24 (top)
 Alexandros Michailidis: p. 44 (bottom)
 Amani A: p. 38
 archna nautiyal: p. 33 (bottom right)
 Arvind Balaraman: p. 29 (center)
 Blake Elliott: p. 12
 Chris Allan: p. 37 (top)
 Cubankite: p. 26 (center left)
 EnclusiveMedia: p. 37 (bottom)
 Featureflash Photo Agency: p. 22 (top)
 Henry C Jorgenson: p. 4
 H.mohammed: p. 26 (bottom)
 Ink Drop: p. 39
 Johnny Silvercloud: p. 40 (bottom)
 Jonathan Weiss: p. 30 (bottom)
 Joseph Sohm: p. 11, 32 (bottom left), 36 (top right)
 kan Sangtong: p. 1

Kevin D Jeffrey: p. 17 (green and blue signs)
Kim Kelley-Wagner: p. 7 (top left)
LMspencer: p. 24 (bottom)
Marc Bruxelle: p. 17 (orange and red signs)
mark reinstein: p. 7 (bottom left)
Meeh: p. 27 (bottom)
Nicole Glass Photography: p. 18 (bottom right)
photocosmos1: p. 27 (top right)
R. Bociaga: p. 25 (bottom)
Rebekah Zemansky: p. 32 (bottom right)
Rob Crandall: front cover, p. 7 (top right), 31 (top)
Robi Jaffrey: p. 32 (center left)
Stone s Throwe Photo: p. 5 (top)
Stratos Brilakis: p. 23 (top)
Trong Nguyen: p 7 (bottom right), 43
Vic Hinterlang: p. 13
www.un.org—Screen Shot 2021-08-25 at 2.06.31 PM.png:
 p. 45 (inset)
Wikimedia Commons
 Andrew Scheer: p. 30 (top)
 Knoper: p. 33 (center)
 Leafsfan67: p. 22 (bottom)
 M.husseiny1: p. 25 (top left)
 Ohio Statehouse: p. 21 (top)
 United States Capitol: p. 8–9 (bottom)
 Vadim Savitsky, mil.ru: p. 25 (top right)
 Warren K. Leffler, U.S. News &World Report Magazine:
  p. 34 (bottom)
 Zeyad Al-Enezi: p. 26 (top right)
 Zorion: p. 33 (top)
All other images from Shutterstock

Crabtree Publishing Company

www.crabtreebooks.com   1-800-387-7650

Printed in the U.S.A./072022/CG20220201

Published in Canada
Crabtree Publishing
616 Welland Ave.
St. Catharines, Ontario
L2M 5V6

Published in the United States
Crabtree Publishing
347 Fifth Ave
Suite 1402-145
New York, NY 10016

Library and Archives Canada Cataloguing in Publication
Available at the Library and Archives Canada

Library of Congress Cataloging-in-Publication Data
Available at the Library of Congress

Hardcover: 9781039663336   Paperback: 9781039663824
Ebook: 9781039668256   Epub: 9781039685659
Read-along: 9781039686144   Audio book: 9781039668744

Contents

INTRODUCTION   4

CHAPTER 1
Values   8

CHAPTER 2
Democratic Governments   16

CHAPTER 3
Processes   28

CHAPTER 4
In Your Community   38

WRAP UP
Active Citizenship   42

Learn More   45

BIBLIOGRAPHY   46

GLOSSARY   47

INDEX   48

About the Author   48

Introduction

What comes to mind when you hear the word "democracy"? Do you picture a country or a government? Or do you think about voting or the freedom to choose who and what represents you and your values? Democracy stands for all these things, so it can be difficult to define.

Democratic Government

A government is a political system that **regulates** and runs a country or community. The many parts of a modern democratic government work together to serve its citizens. People vote to choose who will speak and act for them. This is known as representative democracy because these leaders represent the people. Chapter 2 is an overview of how the democratic governments in the United States and Canada work. It also describes other forms of government.

Like many cities, Milwaukee, Wisconsin, uses absentee ballot boxes for people who cannot vote in person. During elections, they are located at safe sites throughout the city. The SafeVote drop boxes are staffed and have cameras watching them to ensure there is no tampering with the votes. Free and fair elections are important for healthy democracies.

Democratic Processes

Democracy also relates to processes. These are sets of steps taken to meet certain goals. **Civic duties** such as paying taxes, serving on **juries**, and voting are all democratic processes. They help a society run smoothly. The processes of the many different parts of democratic governments help citizens, too. They each serve people in distinct ways. Democracy can also have an effect on decision-making. For instance, people share information about an issue, examine it together, and come to an agreement in the deliberative process. This is a process in which information is shared before decisions are made. Learn more about American and Canadian processes in Chapter 3.

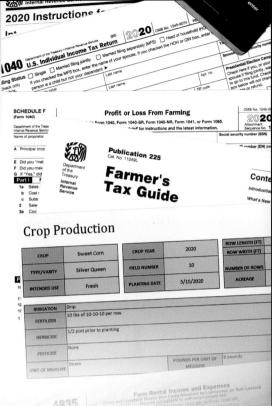

A jury examines all the evidence presented in a court case to determine a verdict.

Democratic Values

Democratic governments and processes are based on shared ideals. These ideals are similar in democracies throughout the world today. Instead of people looking out just for their own interests, they are expected to act together for the common good. This means doing what works best for as many people as possible. However, everyone is free to make their own choices. The majority, or larger group, of voters hold the power in a democracy. Fairness is an important principle. That is why laws are in place to protect the people who are in the minority, or smaller group. The next chapter describes democratic values in more detail. Ways to take part in democracy in your own community are at the end of the book. Keep reading to see how you can take part in democracy!

Democracy in Action

Student Government and Leadership

Student government highlights some of the main aspects of democracy. Schools often choose student leaders at the beginning of the school year. These leaders act on behalf of their classmates. At a middle school, some kids think there should be less homework. Others want better school lunches. Changing the dress code is important to another group. One **candidate**, Carlie, promises to stand up for all of their interests. She also has a plan for other students to advise her. She gets the most votes and wins the election. While in power, Carlie follows the rules set out by the school. She does her best to serve others well. Carlie also helps settle disagreements. When the students argue over where to go on their year-end trip, she guides the group to look at their options. Then they decide on the best choice for the most people. At the end of her **term**, many of Carlie's classmates agree that they would vote for her again!

Student governments share some of the same values and processes as larger governments.

Defining Democracy

A list of common terms

Citizen A person who is legally recognized to have the privileges, or rights, of those who were born in or live in a particular place

Constitution The foundational laws that guide a country

Election A vote in which someone is chosen to hold a certain position

Parliament Assembly of representatives who have been elected to serve

Political party A group of people who work together to get like-minded candidates elected

Representative democracy A government that is chosen by citizens who vote for leaders to represent them

System Parts that work together to meet a common purpose

CHAPTER 1
Values

**Human rights are strongly linked to liberal democracy.
These rights are the basic freedoms every person is born with.**

The United Nations (UN) lists 30 rights in its Universal Declaration of
Human Rights. Introduced in 1948, the UN describes this document as
"a yardstick by which we measure right and wrong" around the world.
The right to equality is a key feature of **liberal democracy**. This is a set
of beliefs based on the rights and freedoms of individuals. It gained
prominence in the late 1600s through the 1700s in Europe, during a time
called The Age of Enlightenment. That was an era when people began to
question the way they were governed. At the time, most governments
were monarchies ruled by kings or queens, and the interests of the wealthy
and **privileged** were most important. In liberal democracies, all people are
seen to have equal value, so they should have the same opportunities in life.

The United Nations has members from 193 countries that work together on global issues. The UN headquarters is located in New York.

In 1939, the 150th anniversary of the Constitution, the U.S. Congress commissioned artist Howard Chandler Christy to paint the signing of the Constitution.

Rights Guaranteed in Writing

Protection against discrimination is a related human right. Discrimination is poor treatment of a group or person that is based on things such as race, **gender**, age, or disability. Democratic countries usually have their own written list of citizens' rights. The United States has the Bill of Rights, for example. Canada has the Canadian Charter of Rights and Freedoms. Upholding these rights helps to shape a democratic government and its processes.

Rights as Democratic Values

Some of the other human rights defined by the UN and upheld by most democracies include:

Article 3: Everyone has the right to life, liberty, and security of person.

Article 4: No one shall be held in slavery.

Article 6: Everyone has the right to recognition everywhere as a person before the law.

Article 7: All are equal before the law and are entitled without any discrimination to equal protection of the law.

Article 13: Everyone has the right to leave any country, including his own, and to return to his country.

Article 19: Everyone has the right to freedom of opinion and expression.

Article 21: Everyone has the right to take part in the government... directly or through freely chosen representatives...The will of the people shall be the basis of the authority of government; this will shall be expressed in periodic and genuine elections.

Article 26: Everyone has the right to education.

Check It Out!

Complete UN Universal Declaration of Human Rights:

www.un.org/en/udhrbook/pdf/ udhr_booklet_en_web.pdf

Think About It!

A democracy should protect its citizens against discrimination. Why do you think discrimination still exists in places like the United States and Canada?

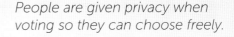

People are given privacy when voting so they can choose freely.

Accountability and Elections

A central pillar of democracy is that citizens hold the power. Governments are **accountable** to them. The media is free to report on what leaders say and do. Voters can show that they approve—or disapprove—when they choose who represents them in the future. Elections must take place regularly. In Canada, for example, federal elections are held on the third Monday in October every four years. American presidential elections take place every four years on the first or second Tuesday in November. Democracies are supposed to encourage all citizens to take part. Adults from all backgrounds have the right to run as candidates. Canadian and American citizens who are at least 18 years old can vote. This is a major responsibility. Who they elect may change the main concerns of their government. Informed voters make their own decisions.

Economic Freedom

Democratic values can also influence an economy. This is a system in which services are offered and goods are made, then they are sold and bought. In a liberal democracy, the government does not have total control over a country's economy. This protects people's liberty, which is the state of being free. Citizens can own businesses and property with limited restrictions or government controls. Being free to choose which kind of job to work at is also a democratic right.

Political Tolerance

Showing tolerance means being open to other people's points of view. This is an essential part of a healthy democracy. Everyone is encouraged to share their opinions. People have the freedom to speak as well as the freedom to object to what is said by others. However, opposing political views need to be considered with respect.

Responsibility of Citizens

To function well, democracies need everyone to do their part. Each citizen is expected to participate. This key principle is linked to democratic processes. For example, adults have specific civic duties, including voting, paying taxes, and serving on juries. They could join or even form political parties. Members of these groups share similar goals for what they want their government leaders to do. People of all ages can take part by being informed about important issues. They can also **petition** and protest to prompt change.

Peaceful public protest or assembly falls under the democratic right to free speech. Some democracies restrict speech rights if they incite, or encourage, hate against groups of people. These people are peacefully protesting the treatment of Indigenous peoples in Canada.

Influencing Lives

Democratic values have positive effects on a society. There are many benefits for citizens. Most importantly, their rights are protected. People do not lose them as governments change. Minorities have equal rights and a voice. Independence gives people the freedom to choose where they live and travel, and who they meet with. They can also decide which jobs they work at and how they promote the common good. Limits on concentrated power help prevent abuse of power that could harm people. When functioning properly, democracies should help ensure government, the military, police, and other leaders are all held responsible for their actions.

A protestor is using his democratic right to free speech and freedom of assembly to call attention to the death of a Black man at the hands of police. He is confronting an officer who is blocking a street. In the United States, public streets, sidewalks, and parks are considered traditional public forums for protests.

Think About It!

The peaceful transfer of power after an election is expected in democracies. How does this reflect democratic values?

13

Pointing to Democracy

The media uses images to signal democratic virtues. Two common symbols are pictures of a voting box and a check mark in a box. These visual cues are linked to free and fair democratic elections. Another well known symbol in democracies is Lady Justice. Lady Justice embodies the concept of the rule of law. This is the democratic principle that all citizens are treated fairly, and subject to the laws of the land. This includes lawmakers and judges. It is often seen in courthouses to show that no one is above the law. Weigh scales are used worldwide as the symbol for democratic justice.

Democracies allow citizens to vote for the elected officials they want to represent them.

Lady Justice is a statue or image of a blindfolded woman. She holds weigh scales in her hand. Based on the Greek goddess Themis and the Roman goddess Justicia, she is portrayed as blindfolded to show that justice should be fair.

Statue of Liberty

Like Lady Justice, the Statue of Liberty is another world-famous figure. France gave the copper statue to the United States in 1886. It was a gift to celebrate the Americans gaining their independence from Britain. The statue stands on Liberty Island in New York City's harbor. Its official name is Liberty Enlightening the World. The torch is meant to light up the path to liberty. Millions of **immigrants** have been greeted by it as they arrive in America. Over the years, the Statue of Liberty became a widely known symbol of democracy. It stands for the values of freedom and independence.

The Statue of Liberty is a symbol of liberty or freedom from tyranny, or unreasonable power yielded by government. Her torch shows how liberty enlightens the world.

Think About It!

What does the Statue of Liberty symbolize to you? Can you think of any similar symbols of democracy in your country?

CHAPTER 2

Democratic Governments

Most systems of government are made up of many parts. The people who form a government are politicians. **They are elected officials. They make laws and** policies. **The public service is the group of mostly unelected workers. They deliver the policies, programs, and services of government. They work alongside and support politicians in many ways.**

A wide variety of departments and institutions make a country's laws. They also uphold its standards and administer, or run, its services. These include courts, social services, the military, education, emergency services, and much more. Democratic and non-democratic governments may have similar systems. However, democracies are founded on the ideals and values described in the previous chapter. Representative democracies, such as the United States and Canada, were designed to work on behalf of their citizens.

The U.S. Capitol is another widely known symbol of democracy. It is where the U.S. Congress meets and makes laws.

Party Politics

Democratic governments do not follow one single model. They share some common traits, though. For example, voters must be able to choose from at least two political parties in national elections. Members of these groups work to help people from their party get elected. This increases their representation in government. Most candidates who are up for election belong to political parties. They get help with their **campaigns** from their party. Voters also have a good idea about which issues are important to candidates based on who supports them. In the United States, the Democrats and Republicans are the two major parties. There are also many minor parties. Five parties regularly hold **seats** in the Canadian Parliament. They are the Liberals, Conservatives, New Democratic Party, Bloc Quebecois, and the Green Party. There are more than 20 registered political parties.

Election campaign signs from different ridings in a Canadian **federal** election. A riding is an electoral district in a parliamentary government.

Power to the People

In addition to having multiple political parties, democracies must keep the government separate from religion. This is often called the separation of church and state. It gives citizens religious freedom. A certain set of beliefs cannot influence everyone's daily lives. Military control is another area where people hold the ultimate authority. A democracy's military is overseen by the government. That means the military is accountable to citizens instead of having power over them. Citizens hold the military responsible for its actions.

Flawed Democracies

The key features of democratic governments described in this chapter are what full democracies look like. These governments work as they should. Many places do not function quite so ideally. Flawed democracies face one or more problems, such as a lack of accountability, or responsibility not being taken for actions.

Some democracies are flawed, or have democratic systems, values, and beliefs, but need to improve. Flawed democracies use voter suppression to influence the results of an election. That could include any number of things, including passing laws preventing certain people from voting, or making it hard for people to register to vote or travel to polling stations.

Constitutional Democracies

A constitution is a set of basic laws that guides a country. In a liberal democracy, it upholds democratic principles, or beliefs and values. The rights of individuals are key highlights. The laws protect and apply equally to all citizens. A constitution also assigns roles for the parts of a government and how they work together. Democratic governments' powers are limited. They have enough authority, or power, to do their duties, but cannot abuse it for their own gain. A country's constitution is usually a formal written record. It is a "working document" that can be amended or changed. Amendments follow strict rules. They can only be made by a majority agreement. The Constitution of the United States has been amended 27 times since it came into effect in 1789. Some democratic countries, such as the United Kingdom, have uncodified constitutions. That means there is no single written document. Instead, the constitution is a collection of laws found in a variety of sources. Countries that are not democratic can have constitutions as well.

On April 17, 1982, Queen Elizabeth II signed the proclamation that brought Canada's Constitution Act, 1982, into effect.

Case Study

The Canadian Constitution

In 1867, the British Empire passed the *British North America Act*. This Act formed Canada from some of Britain's North American **colonies**. It later became known as the *Constitution Act, 1867*. Prime Minister Pierre Trudeau worked with provincial leaders to craft a new act in the early 1980s. They wanted something that would be easier for the Canadian government to amend. When the second *Constitution Act* was introduced in 1982, the country gained its independence. It then had the power to change its rules without British permission. The *Canadian Charter of Rights and Freedoms*, which protects all citizens, including Indigenous peoples, was also added. These important documents include rules for the government. The Canadian constitution is not a single written document. For more than 150 years, Canada has followed many of the same unwritten rules that are widely accepted in the United Kingdom. For example, the powers of the Canadian prime minister are not outlined in writing, unlike those of the American president.

CANADIAN CHARTER OF RIGHTS AND FREEDOMS

Whereas Canada is founded upon principles that recognize the supremacy of God and the rule of law:

Guarantee of Rights and Freedoms

The *Canadian Charter of Rights and Freedoms* guarantees the rights and freedoms set out in it subject only to such reasonable limits prescribed by law as can be demonstrably justified in a free and democratic society.

Fundamental Freedoms

Democratic Rights

Mobility Rights

Legal Rights

Equality Rights

Official Languages of Canada

Minority Language Educational Rights

Enforcement

General

Application of Charter

Citation

P.E. Trudeau 1981

Check It Out!

https://laws-lois.justice.gc.ca/eng/const/page-12.html

Direct Democracies

The term "democracy" has its roots in the **city-states** of ancient Greece, such as Sparta and Athens. Athens was run by a direct democracy. The non-enslaved, male population had the right to decide on laws and customs together. They represented themselves directly. This form of democracy still exists. For example, citizens in some small towns in New England all meet to agree on things that affect the community. They have made decisions together this way since the 1700s. Places with thousands—or millions—of citizens make direct democracy impossible. This is why it has been mostly replaced by representative democracy. Citizens choose politicians to represent them and speak for them. Whoever receives the majority of votes becomes the representative who acts on their behalf. Those representatives are called different names in different countries and levels of government.

Cleisthenes was an ancient Athenian lawmaker who is considered a "father of democracy." He increased the power of the Athenian citizens' assembly and decreased the power of the powerful families who wanted to rule.

The Pnyx is a hill in Athens, Greece. As far back as 507 BCE, ancient Athenians held democratic assemblies there. Pnyx means "tightly packed together." Over time, the site was built up with walls, an auditorium, and speaker's platform.

Think About It!

How might relationships among voters affect direct democracy?

Constitutional Monarchy

Representative democracies do not all look the same. For example, Canada is a constitutional monarchy. A monarchy is led by the head of a royal family. Constitutional monarchies share power with an elected government. The amount of influence a monarch has varies. Queen Elizabeth II is Canada's head of state. She is represented across the country by a governor general and provincially by lieutenant governors. The queen yields, or gives, her power to the Canadian government, which controls its own laws. Canada has a parliamentary system. In this form of government, the political party with the most elected representatives holds power. The government is led by a prime minister from that party. This system was copied from what was done in Britain. It is used in many former colonies.

Queen Elizabeth II is Britain's longest serving monarch. She took the throne in 1952. She is Canada's head of state.

The Canadian House of Commons chamber is divided by a central aisle. The Speaker of the House sits on the north end next to the flag. Government members sit on the Speaker's right and opposition members on the left.

Presidential Republic

Like Canada, the United States is a representative democracy. However, the US has a totally different style of government. It is a **republic** with a presidential system. An elected president is the head of state as well as the head of the government. This leader holds more power than one governing in a parliamentary system. Whereas Canadians choose a political party whose leader becomes prime minister, Americans choose the person they want to represent them. In semi-presidential republics, such as France, the president shares power with a prime minister. Their roles are defined by the constitution in each country.

In 2020, Joe Biden got more than 80 million votes—more than any other U.S. presidential candidate in history. The American president is head of state and head of government.

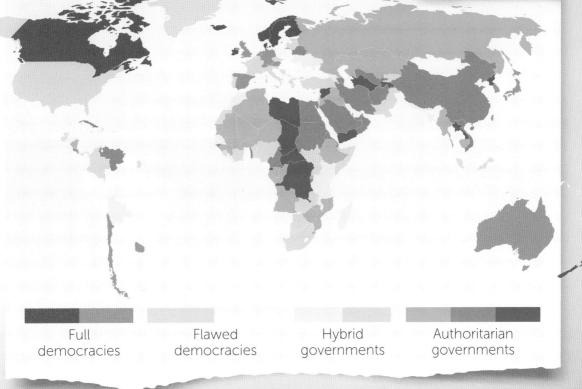

Democracies and Other Forms of Government Throughout the World

Full democracies

Flawed democracies

Hybrid governments

Authoritarian governments

Non-Democratic Governments

There are more than 190 countries around the world. Each one has its own values, government systems, and processes. Less than half of them are democratic. This number includes full and flawed democracies. Some countries claim to be democratic. They may even use the word "democratic" in their name. However, the leaders do not represent their citizens. In fact, they often do not act in their best interests. Constitutions and laws may exist in these places. They do not focus on democratic principles, though. North Korea, for example, is officially called the Democratic People's Republic of Korea. However, just one political party has been in power since 1948. Kim Il-sung controlled the country from that year until he died in 1994. Since then, his son and grandson have held power. Human rights and freedoms are not respected by the North Korean government.

Kim Jong-un is the Supreme Leader of North Korea, like his father and grandfather before him.

Giant statues of Kim Il-sung and Kim Jong-il, dominate a square in Pyongyang, North Korea.

Isaias Afwerki, president of Eritrea

General Min Aung Hlaing of Myanmar

Autocratic Rule

In autocratic governments, total authority is held by one person. Autocratic leaders use their power to defeat anyone who opposes them. They are often referred to as dictators. The United Nations has described Eritrean President Isaias Afwerki as an autocratic leader. He has ruled the African country with no elections since 1993. Autocracies often use military forces to control citizens. In some cases, the military itself heads the government. This is is called a military dictatorship. It may come into power through a coup. A coup occurs when a military illegally overthrows, or brings down, a government. General Min Aung Hlaing seized control of Myanmar this way in 2021.

Autocratic governments maintain power through fear and force. Some are called "police states." They use extreme levels of monitoring and control over people.

Absolute Monarchies

Another form of autocracy is an absolute monarchy. More than 24 monarchies exist around the world today. These rulers often inherit their positions. The monarchs in some of these kingdoms, such as Saudi Arabia, hold total power over their subjects. They can do as they wish without being accountable to the people.

Salman bin Abdulaziz Al Saud, king of Saudi Arabia

Mohammed bin Salman Al Saud is Salman bin Abdulaziz's son. He is the Crown Prince of Saudi Arabia and controls his father's government. He has made some reforms, such as removing a ban on women drivers. But his family's rule is still very strict and does not allow people to disagree.

Authoritarianism

Governments that do not consult with or welcome input from citizens are authoritarian. This includes absolute monarchies and military dictatorships. Other authoritarian governments are based on a shared set of political beliefs. Communism is a significant example. This system places all aspects of public life under the government's control. Citizens of China, for instance, are under control of their country's Communist Party. Totalitarianism is an extreme form of authoritarianism. Citizens cannot express their opinions or defy the government in any way.

Xi Jinping is president of the People's Republic of China (PRC).

民共和国万岁　　世界人民大团

Authoritarian governments need the support of strong armies to carry out their will.

CHAPTER 3

Processes

A democratic government has processes that help it serve its citizens well. Some of these processes relate to civic duties. These include serving on juries, paying taxes, and voting in elections. Others focus on making decisions and preserving the rule of law. A closer look at how a democracy works reveals multiple complex systems. These parts and processes keep it running smoothly.

Levels of Government

Like many democracies, the United States and Canada use the federal system. That means they have three levels of government: national, state or provincial/territorial, and municipal. They all work together on their citizens' behalf. Each has its own duties and processes. Towns and cities are part of the municipal, or local, level. They may be grouped together into counties, districts, or regions. This level controls community services such as parks, libraries, and police forces. State or provincial governments have more authority. They handle decisions about education, health care, and other major areas. The national level is also known as the federal government. It oversees things that affect the entire nation.

Think About It!

Different levels of government are responsible for different things. Can you name some things they work together on?

Municipal/Local

State/Provincial/Territorial

Federal/National

First responders operate through municipal, or local, levels of government.

The regulation of higher education often falls under state or provincial governments.

The military is a federal government responsibility.

Government Branches

Each level of a democratic government is often split into three branches, or parts with distinct roles. These are commonly known as the executive, legislative, and judicial branches. At the federal level, the executive branch in the United States includes a president, who leads the country. Governors lead at the state level. In Canada, the prime minister leads the country at the federal level. **Premiers** lead at the provincial or territorial level.

In all levels of government, the legislative branch includes elected members of government. They work together to make laws and **policies**.

In Canada, premiers are the leaders of provincial/territorial governments.

A legislative assembly is a group of elected representatives.

Judicial Branch

The judicial branch is the court system. It interprets the laws made by the other branches. Many court cases are ruled on by state or provincial courts. Depending on the dispute, cases can move all the way up to a country's Supreme Court. This body is formed by a group of appointed judges. People who are appointed are not elected by citizens. Instead, they are chosen by political leaders. For example, Canadian senators in the federal legislative branch are appointed by the governor general. This is done with the prime minister's support.

The examples in this chart are for the United States and Canada. Most other federal democracies have similar levels and branches. They may use different terms, however.

John G. Roberts, Jr., Chief Justice of the United States

Government Level	Executive Branch	Legislative Branch	Judicial Branch
Federal	President/ Prime Minister	Member of Congress/ Member of Parliament	Supreme Court Justices
State/Provincial/ Territorial	Governor/Premier	Legislative Representatives	State/Provincial Judges
Municipal	Mayor	Councillors	Municipal Judges (U.S.)

Supreme Court of Canada

The Lower Nicola Indian Band of the Nlaka'pamux First Nations in British Columbia, Canada, signed an agreement with the province and a mining company to share revenues from a mine located on band territory. This is an example of collaboration between levels of government.

Public Service

Each level and branch of a democratic government employs people who carry out its work. These include elected representatives and the public service. People who work in public service have a huge variety of jobs in many areas. They keep their positions as the politicians they work alongside are voted in and out. Depending on their roles, public servants may advise political leaders and help them make decisions. They are an important group in democracies because they can keep governments accountable.

Making and Keeping Laws

Democracies all have their own processes for making laws. A draft of a proposed law is called a bill. In general, a bill is introduced at the legislative level. There are usually multiple stages of it being read, debated, and amended. This is called a deliberative process. After a bill passes a majority vote, what happens next depends on the government. At the federal level in the United States, for example, the president approves the bill to make it a law. In Canada, the governor general gives it **Royal Assent**.

Interpreting Laws

Sometimes, there are questions about laws and even constitutions. The judicial branch interprets, or decides the meaning of, the laws and makes them clear. People in the various levels and branches of government do not always agree on major legal issues. Citizens may also disagree. It is important to hear everyone's point of view in a democracy. A referendum is a direct vote that can be called to settle disputes. It poses a single question that people vote on. The popular opinion wins.

A 1995 referendum held in Quebec asked citizens of the province if they wanted to separate from Canada. The majority voted against it.

Mary Simon is the first Indigenous governor general in Canada. She is Inuk, born in Kangisualuujjuaq, Quebec.

President Joseph Biden signs a bill to make it law.

Case Study

Brown vs. Board of Education of Topeka

In 1896, the Supreme Court of the United States made a ruling that helped shape the country. It decided that Homer Plessy's rights were not violated by segregating, or keeping apart, the races on train cars. That ruling enforced a "separate but equal" way of life in America. It allowed many civil rights abuses. Public officials used it to defend racist processes.

For example, the Board of Education in Topeka, Kansas, refused to allow Linda Brown to attend a school that was only for white children in 1951. Her father disagreed with their rules. He argued in a state court that his daughter had the right to equality. Brown lost. He then appealed to the U.S. Supreme Court. In 1954, the judges unanimously ruled that segregated public schools defied the 14th Amendment of the Constitution. The way they interpreted the law had a huge impact on American society. The civil rights movement got a huge boost. It led the way for changes at all levels and in all branches of the government.

Linda Brown's case changed schooling in America.

Sometimes governments block democratic reforms. Alabama Governor George Wallace was firm in his belief in segregation. In 1953, President John F. Kennedy ordered an army division to enforce racial integration at the University of Alabama. Governor Wallace stood at the school door in a personal attempt to stop Black students from enrolling.

Some democracies, such as the United Kingdom, use the unitary system. Unlike the federal system, their national government works directly with local leaders.

During the COVID-19 pandemic, some governments had mask mandates. These were official orders, but not laws that required people over a certain age to wear masks indoors. Liberal democracies respect personal freedoms, but act to restrict those freedoms when they pose a threat of harm to others.

Rules and Laws

Citizens are expected to obey laws because they chose the representatives who made them. Democracies follow the rule of law—remember Lady Justice described on page 14? Everyone is held equally accountable to fair rules. This helps prevent abuses of power that are often found in autocracies. It also entrusts citizens with upholding the common good for all.

The rules that people follow, in their community, at work, at school, and at home, each have their own purposes. Laws that are made by a **legislature** and imposed by the judicial branch often protect human rights. For example, they may ensure that someone's constitutional rights are defended. Other laws, such as wearing a seatbelt, or protecting children from working underage, are intended to help keep citizens safe. Rules created by smaller groups meet their own needs. In a classroom, for example, students raise their hands and wait to be called upon by a teacher to prevent everyone from speaking at once. Laws and rules help people resolve conflicts fairly and peacefully. They also make the consequences for breaking them clear and enforceable.

Think About It!

Think of a rule that is important to your teacher or parent. Is it connected to democratic values? What would happen if it was not enforced?

Deliberative Process

The process for making a rule or law is democratic if the will of the people has been done. Deliberative processes are used in a variety of settings. Civil society describes groups that are not governments or businesses. There is a huge range of these networks of people. They include faith-based organizations, community services, environmental activists, and **unions**. Members of these groups can propose a rule or action, consider and judge it together, and decide what to do. Like a government body, they can vote with the majority rules for making decisions. Another way is to get consensus, which is when the group widely agrees. This requires discussion, valuing and considering other people's ideas, and being willing to change opinions.

Powers and Limits

People who live in democracies follow the rule of law and uphold the public good, but they also have plenty of freedom. They can protest, show their dissatisfaction with their government leaders, and start petitions. Ultimately, they can vote their elected representatives out of office. Even while in power, no one leader has total control. For example, the American president can approve and **veto** laws, but not make laws. They cannot be part of the legislative branch. This is made up of the U.S. House of Representatives and the Senate. There are fixed terms for the president and other elected representatives. They must meet citizens' expectations to win future elections.

Parliamentary Style

In Canada, parliament is the name for the federal legislature. It includes the elected House of Commons as well as the unelected Senate. The Senate is the upper house of parliament whose appointed members are intended to review laws and provide "sober second thought." Laws need approval of both houses, but the House of Commons is dominant in practice.

The prime minister and **cabinet** members must be members of parliament. The House of Commons has 338 seats. A political party must win 170 of those to form a **majority** government. With 169 seats or less, it is a **minority** government. Minority governments need the support of other political parties to pass laws. Canadian governments can be thrown out of power if, in a minority government, the majority of representatives in the House of Commons from other parties "lose confidence" in the government and vote against it.

Canadian Prime Minister Justin Trudeau led one majority and two minority parliaments with the Liberal Party.

Black Lives Matter protests highlight injustices while calling for the end of inequality and abuse of power.

CHAPTER 4

In Your Community

If you live in the United States or Canada, you are part of a representative democracy. Your state or province as well as your local community are also democracies. If you live in another place, consider the similarities and differences between your home and what you have read in this book. Remember, democratic values, systems, and processes are not just for governments. They are found in schools, workplaces, and even families!

Investigating Democracy

What does democracy look like in your community? Start exploring it by checking out your local print and online media. Which issues are covered in articles and opinion pieces? Reflect on how they reveal democratic values and principles. Look for stories about what your representatives at each level of government are saying and doing. You could also research how local citizens get involved in elections. Learn about which political parties are in your community and what they support.

Find out whether there are any debates about new rules or laws that affect you or your family. You can assess the health of your democracy, as well. Watch for real-life examples of discrimination and inequality. Consider how tolerant people are of opposing views. Evaluate whether your leaders seem to be serving themselves or the people they represent.

People in the United Kingdom voted to withdraw from the European Union government in 2016. A referendum is a direct vote by voters on a specific issue or proposal. It is a way to directly participate in democracy.

Democracy in Daily Life

Pay attention to who makes the rules that affect your everyday life. Ask questions! Be aware of how you can get involved and be heard. For example, what is your school's policy on students having phones in the classroom? What process led to that decision? Whose voices were heard? Did the students, teachers, school board, and parents try to reach a consensus? Was a vote held? Find out if there are rules in your town or city that treat one group, such as people who are your age, differently than others. If so, how did they come about? Could they be changed?

Think About It!

U.S. Supreme Court Justice Felix Frankfurter is credited with saying, "In a democracy, the highest office is the office of citizen." Is this true in your community or country? Why or why not?

Young people can protest to stand up for themselves. They can also petition their leaders like these youths at a London, U.K. climate march.

Case Study

Student Vote

CIVIX is a Canadian program that aims to strengthen democracy. It does this by educating students. One of its projects is Student Vote, which runs alongside general elections. Elementary and high school classes can take part for free. They receive supplies that inform students about the voting process. They also get the materials needed to run their own elections. First, students research political parties and learn more about the issues. Then they decide which candidates from their area they want to represent them. They are also encouraged to discuss what they learn outside of school. This helps engage their family members in elections. The students vote on the same day as adults. Their results are posted so they can see how well their candidate performed.

Democracy requires constant vigilance. It needs citizens to be aware and to hold governments accountable. This person carries a sign that honors the words of American statesman and civil rights activist John Lewis. On March 1, 2020, he encouraged his fellow citizens to "get in good trouble, necessary trouble, and redeem the soul of America." Lewis's words remember a March 7, 1965, event in which peaceful protestors, including Lewis, were beaten by police for crossing the Edmund Pettus Bridge in Selma, Alabama. They were marching for their democratic voting rights.

Take Action

Citizens in democracies are expected to get involved. They need to put the public good ahead of themselves, while enjoying their freedoms. This takes root in simple acts and decisions at the local level. Basic human rights need to be valued and protected. This is true in homes, schools, and communities. If the majority of people do not protect the rights of those who think or act differently from them, then some citizens are no longer treated equally. Issues with free and fair local elections must be investigated. Politicians need to be held accountable at every level. Conflicts arise when people aren't willing to hear one another's opinions and ideas. Keeping a democracy healthy requires everyone to do their part.

Think About It!

What are some ways your family could practice democratic ideals as you make decisions? What are the pros and cons of reaching a consensus?

Active Citizenship

It is important to understand what democracy is in order to defend it. Governments that abuse human rights, do not follow the rule of law, and do not serve their citizens well may still claim to be democratic.

Even healthy democracies can fail under the right conditions. Voters can stop caring or think that they do not make a difference. Political intolerance can increase. Citizens can lose interest in staying informed. Politicians can refuse to be accountable. To prevent an area or a group from being a democracy in name only, it is essential for people to understand the values, systems, and processes of democracy.

Think About It!

Definitions of democracy vary. After reading this book, how would you explain democracy to someone?

Democracy and You

How does understanding democracy affect you and your community? Now you know that information and action need to come together to uphold its ideals. Being aware of human rights and the principles of democracy helps citizens see when there is a problem. Being ready to jump in and stand up for democracy is the next step. Be openminded and encourage others to follow your lead. Think about whether something is fair and speak out if it is not!

Be an Informed Citizen!

Do you know...

- who your elected leaders are at different levels of government?

- what issues are important to the political parties at each level? How do these issues line up with what is important to you?

- when the next elections will be held locally, in your state or province, and nationally?

Call to Action

Everyone can play a role in upholding democracy and democratic values. Young people are the future. The time to shape what the future will look like is now. Start with an issue that it important to you or your community. Find out what your elected representatives think about it by investigating online or contacting them directly. Consider how you can share your views. To help you get a better understanding, talk with people who have other opinions and beliefs.

Learn More

Build on what you have learned in this book. Use the resources below to research human rights and freedoms, government systems, and democratic processes. Then use your knowledge to take part in democracy!

More details about the CIVIX Student Vote program described on page 40:	**https://studentvote.ca**
Read descriptions of all 30 articles included in the Universal Declaration of Human Rights:	**www.un.org/en/udhrbook/pdf/ udhr_booklet_en_web.pdf**
Get informed about American levels and branches of government:	**www.whitehouse.gov/about-the-white-house/our-government**
Learn more about Canadian democracy through "Explore Our Country, Our Parliament":	**https://lop.parl.ca/About/Parliament/ Education/OurCountryOurParliament/ home-e.aspx**
Discover "How Canadians Govern Themselves":	**https://lop.parl.ca/about/parliament/ senatoreugeneforsey/home/index-e.html**
Find out about the elections process in the United States:	**www.usa.gov/election**
Find out about the elections process in Canada:	**https://electionsanddemocracy.ca/ canadas-elections**

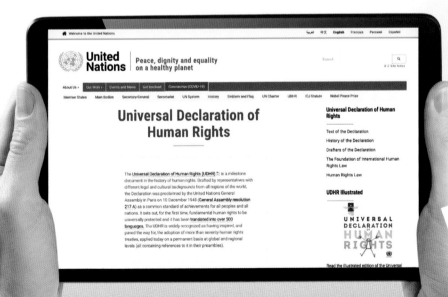

Bibliography

Introduction

"Citizenship Education Resources." *CIVIX* civix.ca/resources

"Defining Democracy." Facing History & Ourselves. https://bit.ly/3zooZmk

Heslop, D. Alan. "political system." *Britannica.* www.britannica.com/topic/political-system

"Political system." *Science Daily.* https://bit.ly/2US7HyU

"The road to democracy." The World's Children's Prize. worldschildrensprize.org/democracy

Chapter 1

"America's Founding Documents." National Archives. www.archives.gov/founding-docs

"Human Rights." Canadian Human Rights Commission. www.chrc-ccdp.gc.ca/en

Rather, Dan. "Do Republicans Believe in Democracy? The press needs to start asking." *Steady*, March 7, 2021. https://bit.ly/3gtoXSw

"Statue of Liberty dedicated." *History.* https://bit.ly/2WqOFQj.

"The Rule of Law." LexisNexis. https://bit.ly/3zvKa61

"Universal Declaration of Human Rights." United Nations. https://bit.ly/3sMW098

Chapter 2

Crawford, Amy. "For the People, by the People." *Slate*, May 22, 2013. https://bit.ly/3gyh2TV

Cuddy, Alice. "Myanmar coup: What is happening and why?" *BBC News.* https://bbc.in/3DkEkq2

Dewey, Caitlin, and Max Fisher. "Meet the world's other 25 royal families." *The Washington Post*, July 22, 2013. https://wapo.st/3zn3S4a

Doerr, Audrey D. "Public Service." *The Canadian Encyclopedia*, December 16, 2013. https://bit.ly/3zhTvOH

"Explore Our Country, Our Parliament." Parliament of Canada. https://bit.ly/38cgZsn

"Global democracy has a very bad year." *The Economist*, February 2, 2021.http://econ.st/3Fi5jlT

Harris, Carolyn. "Constitutional Monarchy." *The Canadian Encyclopedia*, July 27, 2021. https://bit.ly/2XYa7Nx

"How Local Government Works." Association of Municipalities of Ontario. https://bit.ly/3ybq6nS

Misachi, John. "Countries With Uncodified Constitutions." World-Atlas, April 25, 2017. https://bit.ly/3ynwcBO

"parliamentary system." Britannica. www.britannica.com/topic/parliamentary-system

Patrick, John. *Understanding Democracy: A Hip Pocket Guide*. New York, NY: Oxford University Press, 2006.

Shvili, Jason. "What Is Authoritarian Government?" World Atlas, March 25, 2021. https://bit.ly/3zhsjiN

"State and Local Government." The White House. https://bit.ly/2WmBFLQ

Taylor, Adam. "The brutal dictatorship the world keeps ignoring." *The Washington Post*, June 12, 2015. https://wapo.st/2Si8rfa

"The Constitution." The White House. https://bit.ly/38aARML

Chapter 3

"Canada's System of Justice." Government of Canada. https://bit.ly/3gziupj

Ingram, George. "Civil society: An essential ingredient of development." Brookings, April 6, 2020. https://brook.gs/3zlHR5d

"Law and the Rule of Law." Judicial Learning Center. https://bit.ly/3zjwVoP

"Presidential Election Process." USAGov. www.usa.gov/election

Rémillard, Gil, et al. "Supreme Court of Canada." *The Canadian Encyclopedia*. https://bit.ly/38bLs9U

"The vote that toppled Paul Martin's minority government." *CBC*, November 28, 2018. https://bit.ly/3zjsMRN

Chapter 4

Center for Civic Education. www.civiced.org

Linn, Susan, and Alvin Poussaint. "Democracy Begins at Home." Family Education. https://bit.ly/3Dri0vl

"Student Vote." CIVIX. studentvote.ca

Glossary

accountable Being held responsible, or answering for one's actions

cabinet The council that advises leaders such as a prime minister or president

campaigns Competitions by candidates for political office

candidate A person who seeks political office

city-states Cities that are also states or nations, mostly in the ancient and medieval world

civic duties The mandatory duties of citizens, such as obeying laws, paying taxes, and serving on juries

colonies Countries or areas settled and ruled by another country or empire

federal A central government or the overall government of a country

gender A classification based on a person's identity as female, male, both, or other

immigrants People who move to other countries to live

juries Groups of people sworn to give a verdict in court trials

legislature A government body that makes laws

liberal democracy Countries that follow a form of government and a political ideology, or belief system, in which individual freedom is valued. Also known as western democracy

majority The party with the most votes

minority A party that can form a government with less than half the votes but which must rely on the support of other government parties to stay in power

petition A formal written request

politician A person who holds political office

policies Courses of action followed by governments or political parties

premiers The government leaders of provinces or territories in Canada

privileged Having unearned rights or benefits that give some people or groups advantages in life

regulates Controls or directs something

republic A type of government where the head of state is not a monarch and the power rests with the citizens who are allowed to vote

Royal Assent When a representative of the Crown, or monarch, approves a bill, making it into law

seats Geographical areas represented by members of parliament (MP) elected in a parliamentary government

term A period of time in which a government serves

unions Organized associations of workers that are formed to protect and improve workers' rights

veto Reject a bill or law passed by another level of government

Index

A
absolute monarchies 26, 27
abuses of power 13, 18, 19, 34, 35, 37, 42
accountability 11, 13, 18, 26, 32, 35, 40, 41, 42
Afwerki, Isaias 25
Al Saud, Mohammed bin Salman 26
ancient Greece 21
authoritarian/totalitarian governments 23, 27
autocracies 25, 26

B
branches of government 30–31, 32, 33, 34, 35, 36, 27

C
Canada 9, 10, 11, 12, 16, 17, 19, 20, 22, 23, 28, 30, 31, 32, 33, 37, 38, 40
Charter of Rights and Freedoms 9, 20
China 27
civic duties 5, 12, 28
civil rights 34, 40
communities, democracy in 6, 21, 28, 35, 36, 38–41, 43–44
consensus 36, 39
constitutions 7, 9, 19, 20, 23, 24, 33, 34, 35
courts 5, 14, 20, 31, 34, 39

D
deliberative processes 5, 33, 36
dictatorships 25, 27
direct democracy 21
discrimination 9, 10, 38

E
education/schools 6, 10, 16, 25, 28, 29, 34, 35, 39, 40, 41
elections 7, 10, 11, 17, 25, 28, 26, 36, 38, 40, 41

F
federal/national governments 11, 17, 28, 29, 30, 31, 33, 35, 37
flawed democracies 18, 23, 24
forms of government 23
freedoms 4, 8, 9, 10, 11, 12, 13, 18, 20, 24, 35, 36, 41

G
getting involved 41–44

H
human rights 8–10, 20, 21, 24, 34, 35, 41, 42, 43

I
Indigenous peoples 12, 20, 32, 33

K
Kim Jong-un 24

L
Lady Justice 14
laws 6, 7, 14, 16, 18, 19, 21, 22, 24, 30, 33, 35, 36, 42
liberal democracies 8, 11, 19

M
majority and minority governments 37
majority rules 6, 21, 36
military forces 13, 16, 18, 25, 27, 29

monarchies 8, 22, 26, 27
municipal/local government 28, 29, 30, 31, 35

N
non-democratic governments 24
North Korea 24

P
parliaments 7, 17, 22, 23, 37
presidents 11, 20, 23, 25, 27, 30, 31, 33, 34, 36
prime ministers 30, 31, 37
protests 12, 13, 36, 37, 39, 40

R
referendums 33, 38
representative democracies 4, 7, 16, 23, 38

S
Saudi Arabia 26
Statue of Liberty 15
Student Vote/CIVIX 40

U
unitary governments 35
United Kingdom 35, 38
Universal Declaration of Human Rights 8

V
voters/voting 4, 5, 6, 7, 11, 12, 14, 17, 18, 21, 23, 28, 32, 33, 36, 38, 40, 42

About the Author

Rebecca Sjonger is the author of more than 50 non-fiction books for young people. She still remembers which candidate she voted for when she cast her first ballot almost 30 years ago!